A MEMORY

OF THE

FUTURE

A MEMORY OF THE FUTURE

POEMS

ELIZABETH SPIRES

W. W. NORTON & COMPANY

Independent Publishers Since 1923

NEW YORK | LONDON

For information about permission to reproduce selections from this book, write to
Permissions, W. W. Norton & Company, Inc., 500 Fifth Avenue, New York, NY 10110

For information about special discounts for bulk purchases, please contact
W. W. Norton Special Sales at specialsales@wwnorton.com or 800-233-4830

Manufacturing by Versa Press
Book design by JAM Design
Production manager: Beth Steidle

Library of Congress Cataloging-in-Publication Data

Names: Spires, Elizabeth, author.
Title: A memory of the future : poems / Elizabeth Spires.
Description: First edition. | New York : W. W. Norton & Company, [2018] |
Includes bibliographical references.
Identifiers: LCCN 2018004711 | ISBN 9780393651058 (hardcover)
Classification: LCC PS3569.P554 A6 2018 | DDC 811/.54—dc23
LC record available at https://lccn.loc.gov/2018004711

W. W. Norton & Company, Inc., 500 Fifth Avenue, New York, N.Y. 10110
www.wwnorton.com
W. W. Norton & Company Ltd., 15 Carlisle Street, London W1D 3BS

1 2 3 4 5 6 7 8 9 0

in memory of William Gifford

(1928–2015)

CONTENTS

~ ~ ~

Pome

From flowering gnarled trees
they come, weighing down
the branches, dropping
with a soft sound onto
the loamy ground. Falling
and fallen. That's a pome.

Common as an apple. Or
more rare. A quince or pear.
A knife paring away soft skin
exposes tart sweet flesh.
And deeper in, five seeds in a core
are there to make more pomes.

Look how it fits in my hand.
What to do? What to do?
I could give it to you.
Or leave it on the table
with a note both true and untrue:
Ceci n'est pas un poème.

I could paint it as a still life,
a small window of light
in the top right corner

(only a dab of the whitest white),
a place to peer in and watch it
change and darken as pomes will do.

O I remember days . . .
Climbing the branches of a tree
ripe and heavy with pomes.
Taking whatever I wanted.
There were always enough then.
Always enough.

~ ~ ~

There are mountains hidden in marshes,
mountains hidden in the sky.
There are mountains hidden in mountains . . .
mountains hidden in hiddenness.

Mountains and Rivers Sutra

MASTER DŌGEN

life of i

i.

i left the capital   hurrying away   i carried nothing
a dark night before me   a dark dark night
but when morning came   i stood   free & alone
casting a seven-league shadow   west
i would go west   following the only road

ii.

once i lost a ball   it was red   i watched it
bouncing down the street   intent on losing itself
in the tall grass   i dream about it still
& wake up sweating   from the nightmare

iii.

but if i were deprived of sight   of sound
if i lost my head   what would i be?
the question haunts me   how to find myself
when a self is so small   only an iota
of doubt & longing   how to go on?

iv.

a poet who believed in me   is gone
but in his poems   i famously live on

v.

i met a stranger   on the street

she towered over me   she looked familiar

but looked at me   as if i were the stranger

it was like looking   in a funhouse mirror

at a self stretched   beyond all recognition

she looked at me   walked on

v!

if i stand on my head   if i stand on my head

will you say   i am merely   an empty exclamation?

vii.

time is running out   on minutes   years

on what i was   have always been   i only wish

to love   evolve   to not misuse

what i was given   not!

o   little me

Cloud Koan

Clouds have no history, nothing to tell.
Flying above them or through them,
we cannot penetrate their calm demeanor.
Pushed and powered by wind
(or is there a driving force within them?),
they do not resist. We do not resist.
Then turbulence. Turbulence and a flight
through formlessness until, out of nowhere,
a blue-green coast appears, reminding us
the sun never stopped shining. We just didn't know.

Questions, so many questions.
Must one have a name? A face?
Must events be describable?
And what is it like to simply
drift, to have no destination?
One envies an existence
without shame or regret.

As a child I wanted to walk on one,
heights didn't bother me then, but now
I know it would have been impossible,
like walking on the surface of a star.
And so, wandering lonely, I go on

(I *must* go on), like the rain that falls
with a faceless force on what's below,
wondering if this one or that one
were to speak, would its words console
my scattered mind or leave it more bereft?

I

Ink. Ink
on a brush
held by a hand
above me,
beyond me.
Then I am done.
Around me,
white field,
white sky
blending to one.
Where has
the wind gone?
And why is there
no horizon?

Sentry without
a shadow,
I lean a little
but I do not
topple.
To be here.
To be here
is enough.
To say more

would be to say
too much.
Armless, I raise
my arms
to heaven.

Riddle

Puffed like an adder.
Deflated like a balloon.
Tiny or huge, you are
never the right size.

A little man or woman,
you strut, you speak,
you want. You
have delusions.

O little one,
look at yourself,
posturing and ridiculous.
Go now, please go.

But no, without you,
what would I be?
That is the question
I cannot answer

until I am changed into
particle or star, and you,
you drift away as if you
had never been there at all.

I

You stand so straight and tall
and from afar you could be
a column, but up close I can't tell
how tall you are. I run my hands
over your marbly façade,
hug your cool circumference,
and remember, or think I do,
the day you (I mean *I*!) came into
existence. I was on my back,
naked or nearly so, entertained
by waggling *fingers* and *toes*
(I didn't know the words)
when suddenly, toe in mouth,
I put it all together—my first
eureka! moment—and understood
those fleshy nubs were part of me,
and I of them (here the pronouns get
confusing). A shock and a pleasure.
A feeling of power and terror.
I haven't been the same since.

If I climbed you, not an easy thing
to do, I could sit on top of you
the way that flagpole sitters do,
and have a bird's-eye view

of miles and miles around.
So that is what I'll do, hand
over hand I climb and somehow
reach the top only to see
how everyone's thinking aligns
with mine, everyone astride
a pillar of his or her own making,
some near, some far,
some curious, some hostile,
but even so, I wave to all
of them and wait to see
if they wave back.

Zen Sonnet

It was April and we were reading the book about Zen
you were writing your Zen poems and we were talking

about the moment we were in and I was thinking thoughts
that were not Zen: how I know too much too little to teach you

and then I stepped back from each thought and watched it
disappear a horse without a rider over a sharp-edged horizon.

Spring was a pale shade of yellow a green that kept deepening
there was desire and there was a sense of unfolding and I thought

how we can do anything there is no need for an excess of feeling
we can walk through the door that was made for entering and exiting

abandoning the poems that were never ours though we wrote them
to the one who walks into this room when we are gone.

So let us go out into the world and wander a little
beggars with empty bowls in straw hats grass sandals.

The Road

Better a monosyllabic life than a ragged
and muttered one; let its report be short
and round like a rifle, so that it may hear
its own echo in the surrounding silence.
THOREAU

A life: pared to the bone.
Think of a room with no
chair, no bed. Like a monk,

I sit on a black square
in a patch of light.
In my mind, I sit there.

Or, a life on the road
that takes me here, there,
the trees in fall so bare.

And I with just
the rags on my back,
a gnarled stick to lean on.

Your life, held next
to mine, is rich and fat.
You walk with a pack

and wear a big straw hat
that blocks the sun.
You like things loud,

loud songs, and beat
a drum as you walk.
Hoooo there! you call,

but I let you pass.
The days and years
mount up as I walk on

toward a word dark
as night, black as pitch,
still as a held breath.

A place where a night
bird sings. It sounds
like Keats so I stop.

I build a fire,
sleep like the dead,
dream of a bright star,

and wake at dawn,
the sweet bird gone.
Then rise, splash my face

from the stream. Up the road,
a few souls, gray as time,
stand in a patch of shade,

their arms held out.
So it was for this! I think,
This life, this road! This!

and run as I have never
run, back to the beginning,
the very beginning.

They are all
where I left them.
And there is so much to say.

Ensō

zen circles

Thick. Thin.
Open. Shut.
Faint. Dark.
Blurred. Or not.

~ ~ ~

An oval. An oblong.
An orb. Lopsided.
Or a zero that
contains All.

~ ~ ~

In one brushstroke,
one breath, it's done.
Perfectly imperfect.
Or *im*perfectly perfect.

~ ~ ~

Today the paper's blank,
but still I see the ensō,
white on white.

~ ~ ~

Again, what is it?
The face of the unborn.
The face you'll have
when you aren't
you anymore.

~ ~ ~

In the center of
this one: a dot.
Self-portrait
of what I am
and am not.

The Sound of the Sea at the Shore

As one grows older,
there should be fewer
and fewer words to say.

Each one a few letters
but taken together
meaning something large.

Sea. Sun. Shell. I gather
a little pile, burying,
unburying each, or picking

one up and holding it
to the sun, thinking,
too bright, too bright . . .

It is a game without end
that I lose myself in
as the night begins to fall,

and I shiver a little,
my life a colorless cloak
I fancy more and more.

Like a child I will sit here,
refusing all entreaties to
Come in, come in right now . . .

Can words, a single word,
save me or anyone?
I hold one to my ear,

a roaring shell that says
neither yes nor no.
I listen.

Mountains of the Heart

an artist's book drawn by Kameda Bōsai in 1816

If I were to pray a prayer, would the prayer unfold
like a scrolling landscape of mountains, rivers, valleys,
where here, there, a figure sits in calm contemplation,
praying, composing a poem, or just being there,
where a boatman poles his slender craft upstream
against a current trying to take him elsewhere,
or a solitary traveler walks on a winding mountain path,
her cloak wrapped tightly around her, her face obscured.
Here, *here*, and *here*, mountains and the ghost of mountains,
mountains repeating themselves, mountains everywhere,
and playing over, under, and through it all,
the sound of a lonely *qin*, echoing, echoing, echoing.

*

Ink on the page. Ink. In Edo two centuries ago,
on the fifteenth day of the third month, the literati
had a party. Among ink sticks and laughter,
sake and toasts, Bōsai drew deep into the night.
Waking the next morning, wondering, turning
each sheet over, disbelieving, Bōsai asked,
"Who drew these things? Who? Not I, Bōsai.
Not *Old Dullard, Great Fool, Lazybones.*"
And who writes these words that follow me

here, there, like unfamiliar footprints? Who?
Who am I among all this? Surely not the *I*
that stands here now. No, not that I.
If I am anything, I am only *Sage of the Dust,*
Scholar of the Small, Historian of the Drifting Clouds.
But no, even those names are wrong.
Call me *Muddled Ink Carrier, Lost Traveler*
on a Moonless Night, Mute in a Howling Storm.
And you who are here beside me, tell me your name,
not the name of the one who woke in the usual way
this morning, but the name you have always carried,
both precious jewel and lodestone, secretly inside you.
Are you *Heart-Flutterer, Bird Hopping on One Foot,*
Fox Dressed as a Monk? Tell me so that we may
speak freely, from the heart, as we never have before.

*

It grows late, later than it has ever been,
as we pass on narrow mountain passes,
some bravely going forth, some coming back
to places of sad and happy remembrance,
so many paths ascending and descending,
past pines that make a gentle susurration,

whispering to any listeners listening,
Change is unchanging! Change changes all!
I must leave you now among mountains,
as the *qin* plays on and on, its sound advancing
and retreating, both questioning and sure,
while we continue on, the seamlessness
of the present flowing, ever flowing,

                      past us like the barest breeze.

~ ~ ~

What you are looking for is who is looking.

FRANCIS OF ASSISI

Light Like Water

One season bleeds into another.
As rivulets form streams, and streams find rivers,
as rivers lose themselves completely in the sea,
in March, on the first warm day,
we lose ourselves in light. Like rain, it falls
on everyone, the saved and those that aren't
completely sure. *Light like water.*

Face upturned to the sun, the invalid body,
no nurse available, drinks with thirst unquenchable.
Would kneel and give thanks if it could kneel.
The light is merciful, complete.
It falls on graves, soaks deep into the earth,
down and farther down, so that the fingertips of the dead
begin to tingle, are warmed, and touching dry faces,
know they are remembered. *Light like water.*
Tears run down chilly cheeks.
But what do tears mean? Tears are not words,
but tears can speak of things not easily spoken of.

The winter was unending, all void and impasse.
No corpse believes in spring.
Thirst was ever-present, but the word for *thirst* was gone.
But today the children on the playground

fling off their heavy coats. They run through walls
of light as if through waves at a far-off seashore.
They shout. Their voices come and go.
Light like water. The sparrows peck the seeds I scatter
and wait, as we all do, for more. We all want more.

Face upturned to the sun, eyes closed,
like someone very old (*how old am I?*),
I drink it in. *Light like water.*
Stunned by it all, I say
the words over and over
and step into the light again.

They Drive Through Childhood in Their Little Cars

Loving them, we love nothing, no one,
if not change, as they drive through childhood
in their little cars, steering so seriously into the future
while we follow a few steps behind, tripping through
days and weeks and years, watching as they
suddenly speed up, without a glance backward,
                              without waving goodbye.

Not to grow older! Not to grow up!
Once, safe in my kingdom of cocoa, I wished
for that, but years pushed me roughly out the door.
I drove away in my little silver car, gripping
the wheel too tightly, steering so seriously
into the future, without a glance backward,
                              without saying goodbye.

Older now, we know, if we know nothing else,
that we love them as they were, and are,
though what they are keeps changing. We can't keep up.
How seriously they pedal their little cars into a future
we won't be part of. In a moment, a turn ahead
will take them out of sight as we follow, follow for dear life,
                              practicing our goodbyes.

The Amiable Child

ERECTED TO THE MEMORY

OF AN AMIABLE CHILD,

ST. CLAIRE POLLOCK,

DIED 15 JULY 1797

IN THE FIFTH YEAR OF HIS AGE.

private gravesite in Riverside Park, Manhattan

Not a bad place, this. Someone has planted bulbs.
The daffodils are up and spiky blue and purple hyacinth.
Smaller, humbler violets lie low to the ground.
The buds on the overhanging trees are poised
and ready, a green that will deepen as the weeks go on.
Small birds resist a formal gathering, perch
on trembling branches to ask, *Who's here?*
but nobody answers. No, nothing remarkable,
just a child's grave on the cliffs above the river.

It happened on a morning in July.
A small boy running across a long lawn, his shadow
hurrying him on, matching him stride for stride,
pulling him closer, ever closer, to the shining river.
An exclamation of joy, joy and then surprise as his foot
met the cliff's edge, a small life tripping, slipping
so easily into death . . .

I keep coming back. I don't know why.
I have cleared away dead leaves, reaching as far
as I can reach into enclosed and sacred space,
waiting without knowing what I wait for.
These commonplace flowers? These particular
birds, alert and quick to the moment?
If he inhabits this place, these woods (*he does*),
he would notice everything.
A child, it was written, amiable to the end.

March: St. John the Divine

New York

At noon, just as the bells began to ring,
the white peacock spread its rippling tail, the sound
like a sibilant wind rushing through many leaves.

Three of us watched. A dark-haired woman clapped
at the spectacle, and a Spanish man asked for the name
in my language, then held out his arms and said, "I love you."

The peacock turned full circle, then turned again.
It arched its head and cried, cried out, waiting
for an answering cry. But no cry came.

These Lenten weeks are wordless, gray, and slow.
One waits for a sign that never comes, and then it does.
While out on Amsterdam the traffic never slowed,

and people on the sidewalk, each alone,
hurried to wherever it was they were going,
not paying attention, just talking on their phones.

The Streaming

MASSACRE in bold headlines as you walk into the coffee shop.
The news. Constantly streaming. Finding you wherever you are:

At home. In the car. In the grocery store or running in an endless loop
high above Times Square. The not-looking at what screams to be

looked at: the missing ones, the dead, the fires and the bombings,
everything ravaged, burned, cracking in a godless desert heat.

Or closer, moving closer in. On the streets, the homeless,
so many of them, hands held out. A dollar changing hands.

Or, the turning away. The refusal. The hardening as more and more
hold out their hands. The mail. The solicitations. A voice asking you to
    give,

please, won't you give more? And everywhere the ringing of the
phones.
On trains. In waiting rooms. At parties. Weddings. Funerals.

And once, during the third act of a play, an actor alone on the stage,
head bowed, waiting in fury for the endless ringing to end.

Voices saying: *I can't talk to you now.* Or talking on and on.

And you hearing every word: *I am in Baltimore. L.A. Spokane. New York.*

I don't know where I am. I just had lunch. I am getting on the plane. I will see you tonight. Or, Not tonight. Not ever again.

The needing-cessation but nothing ever ceasing. The wanting to scream but not screaming. But today, a space of silence

in a church where figures kneel and pray their pain may cease: *Lord, take away the pain.* Among flickering candles, they pray.

Shattered. Shattered by a ringing phone. But still you pray. Leaving, you pass a girl standing in the shadowed nave.

Holding a book bag tightly to her chest. As if it were a shield. Two words on it, only two words: **STAY HUMAN**.

Pigeon 7 A.M.

Flutter and flurry of wings, the spirit descends
outside a window on the Upper East Side.
Gray note on a gray scale,
the same sound over and over:
ooo ooo   ooo ooo

Me here. You there.
Apprehended but unseen.
There, on the other side of the window.
You are Presence. You are Companionship
without the burden of speaking.

O Great Consoler, I listen in silence
as you have always listened in silence.
How can I accept your silence?
Forgive you your silence?
I forgive you because the spirit
(which is and is not You) is crying:
ooo ooo   ooo ooo

You are so often silent.
But the creature outside the window,
holy or unholy, is not silent. No.
It repeats to whoever will listen:
Not alone. No.

If it left, if You left, what then?
All over the city, the spirit,
making the selfsame sound, descends.

On Riverside Drive

This statue depicts Shinran Shonin (1173–1262) as he appeared propagating the teaching. The statue originally stood in Hiroshima 2.5 kilometers northwest from the center of the first atomic bomb attack. Having survived the full force of the bomb, the statue was brought to New York in 1955 . . .

THE NEW YORK BUDDHIST CHURCH

What is devotion?
These roses left at your feet by a passing pilgrim?
This walk I take each morning where I pause
for a moment, stare up at you
in your missionary's hat and robes,
and offer a silent greeting?

In this wind, waves on the river
ripple backward to their source.
The infolded petals of the rose bend
backward as clouds stream overhead.
The traffic on the parkway streams.
Day and night, it streams without meaning.
And the pilgrim, without thinking, retraces
her steps, rising, moving, coming back,
each day an act of devotion.

As a young man, you practiced the austerities.
But after twenty years you turned
from renunciation to find, in not seeking,
what you sought. Centuries passed.
Your followers cast you in bronze.
You witnessed devastation.
Now pilgrims half a world away
leave roses at your feet.

How wordlessly you stand here,
always the same, never the same.
Your gaze takes in some middle ground
                              I try to live in.
Again I ask, what is devotion?
And again you do not answer.
But no answer is my answer
for today. As I pass on.

Small as a Seed

In despair, do not despair.

KARL RAHNER

In everything, its opposite.
In terror, calm.
In joy, attendant sorrow.
In the sun's ascendancy, its downfall.
In darkness, light not yet apprehended.

At night in bed, I fear the falling off.
Though falling, I will rise.
I fear. Fall arriving now.
In any word so small, the world.
In the world I walk in, a wild wood.

She Leans

after a photograph by A. Aubrey Bodine

A house: scoured and scarred by wind, its unpainted
boards aligned in contrasting verticals of dark and light,
with a chimney that leans a little as the house leans.
Four broken-out windows on facing sides
allow a bird, many birds, to fly easily in and out,
like a mind in the midst of its own vacancy, trying
and failing to hold onto its own rapid, chattering thoughts.

A house unto itself that leans but does not fall.
Being but never doing (*is being enough?*),
storied and memoried (*or has it forgotten everything?*),
does it wonder why that florid, overdramatic sky
can never make up its mind what it wants to do?
Or what happens to those pink and purple clouds
when they drop over the razor-thin horizon?

Taking it all in, coming back to it day after day,
moving toward it and then moving away, walking
in cautious clockwise circles around it, then walking
widdershins, peering curiously into its endless gloom,
stepping over the doorframe into a perfectly empty room
(*no, not empty, there's a curling calendar from 1952*),
do you think it has nothing to do with you? Do you?

Island Graveyard

Deer Isle, Maine

—An inchworm inches across a broken marker
where two families, eight in all, have kept each other company
for a long time, their family plot no bigger than a bedroom,
fenced in by ancient pine trees that give a little shade
and keep out rain. A rusty gate that hangs half off its hinges,
and looks exactly like the headboard of a bed, admits
whoever comes without discrimination, though visitors are rare
in a place where death is writ in lowercase, part of a landscape
of fallen trees gone soft, of lichens bleaching to white,
of old-man's-beard hanging like fancy lacework from all
the trees, swaying whenever the wind blows, but today is still.

~ ~ ~

Their century gone, they lie here and lie here and lie here,
the *Billings* and the *Toothakers*—*Hattie* and *David* and *Mellie*,
Melvina and *William* and *Angenett* and *Lucy* and *John*.
The day is hot, the ground is cool and spongy, and it would be
easy, easy but not wise, to lie down for a moment among them,
the swollen ground my pillow, and wake with a start to nightfall,
the owl alive and hunting, darkness over all . . .

                                               Crow calls to crow,
summoning me back from a place that is not a place at all,
and little by little, the inchworm, better than clock or sundial,

traverses the mossy stones, gathering itself into a ~ ~ ~ ~ ,
then flattening into a line, as if to mend a thread that keeps
unraveling and shape the story into *beginning, middle, end.*

~ ~ ~

Someday you and I will lie formal and lofty in a grave,
the way that speechless effigies of kings and queens
are laid out, side by side, in dim cathedrals for pilgrims
to touch and wonder at. In chaste repose, no longer
will we feel the press of time pour madly through our fingers,
too fast, too fast! What will we feel then, if we feel at all?
Grave tenderness toward a world that goes on easily without us?
Or will the bodiless part of ourselves escape and spread
like smoke until we're nowhere and everywhere at once,
a dispassionate blue curve above a curving planet, like a lens
fitted to an eye that cannot close, that sees too much, sees
more than it wants to see. Crow and cicada won't tell me
what I need to know. *Hattie* and *David* and *Mellie* won't tell me.
And so I read their names the way the inchworm does, by *touch,*
lichen and moss cool against my cheek, green crumbling tendrils
waiting to break me down so slowly I won't even know.

~ ~ ~

This is as good a place as any to be buried, here on an island
caught in a pocket of time, where fog obscures the morning
until the sun breaks through, and the sound of the ocean breaking
against rock draws us farther than we intended until we stand
at water's edge and can go no farther, or going farther say goodbye
to everything we know. Practiced in our farewells, we'll leave
the dead to murmuring posthumous conversations where
racing seasons and constellations figure, where centuries
pass like days and days like centuries, as we retrace our steps
on a path veined and gnarled as an old man's face —
                              Something is creeping up my arm!
An inchworm on my sleeve measuring me for new clothes.

Magicicada

name for the seventeen-year cicada

Lord, when I am taken, will they put me in the ground?
Will I dream the Eternity Dream over and over,
I who am so alone?
Perfectly dead, will I be an *I* then?
Will I welcome holy darkness or wait in vain
for light to strike my face and warm it?
And will I apprehend familiar or unfamiliar footsteps
treading above me on hallowed ground?

    * * *

I remember when the cicadas came.
We had been warned but no warning
could prepare us for the tens of thousands
tunneling upward, emerging from hard shells,
their bulging eyes bright red, their bodies black.
Stunned by light and time, at first they made no sound.
Then, wings unfolding, they rose and joined
the humming swarm. For weeks they sang.
Their song was not a song we knew.
It filled the days and nights unceasing.
It was not human. And then it stopped.
They left gold carapaces behind.
They left a silence in the mind
that deepens as the years go on.

*   *   *

Seventeen years!
Deep in the earth there is no ticking time.
They sleep like tiny gods below us,
blind, sucking on roots, as we continue on,
careless and preoccupied. Sweeping them up,
I marveled they were ever here
and wondered, as I do now,
Will I see them again? Will I?

Gold Bug

Under the chair:
old poems that scroll
back through the years.

Down on my knees, I dig
through drafts of past lives.
Something's alive!

Smaller than an *o*,
a tiny beetle quietly
lives there among words.

The room is dry
as a bone, with no
stray crumb to feast on.

So, scarab, how do you survive?
Yes, that is the question.
How to go on.

My breath, measured
and careful, blows you gently
off the page to land

on the swirling patterned carpet.

Gold on gold now.

Where you continue.

~ ~ ~

You can dive into the past and emerge into the future.

HUAIYEN

The Shrine

I was taken underground   down many flights of stairs
to a room inside the earth   lit by a sourceless light
where   on a rough-hewn pedestal   carved from an ancient
tree   a face stared out at me   stared past me into Time
someone had made the shrine   a woman   I thought
like me   her gray hair wild unkempt   as she worked
the wood with gold   to make a precious overlay
the shrine a place to kneel   & pray for continuance
like a gift   another morning came   cool & gray
bringing the chance of rain   rain that would wash the earth
clean of the summer's dust   but I cannot forget
the shrine   the face   the woman working wonders
buried so deep beneath me   in a room   in the center of the earth

Dream Interrupted—

The earth has many levels,
and escalators descend.
Figures are moving downward,
mother and father and friend.

So many are going down,
quietly, without a word.
One day they are here among us,
and the next they have disappeared.

They eat a last meal before leaving,
a supper of wine and bread.
And bowl after bowl of soup
to prepare themselves to be dead.

I serve and I sit among them.
I eat the proverbial bread.
Soon I will go down with them
to the speechless land of the dead.

Now I clear the plates from the table.
I sweep up the crumbs of bread.
But when I turn back to join them,
they have silently gone ahead.

Is it coldness or kind consideration,
that made them leave as they did?
Leaving me here among the living,
not alive but not quite dead.

Constructing a Religion

Not the rising sun,
but the setting sun.
Not the father,
but the mother.

Not the cross,
but the circle,
drawn in ink,
not blood.

The Word
inhabited
but unspoken,
like a bell unrung.

A cathedral
of the mind,
gray and cool
as Time,

with doors
so tall and heavy
that I must
tug and tug.

Inside, marvels
and terrors
annealed in
bright windows,

and a bird
sheltering in
high hidden spaces,
looking down

on a soul,
small, so small,
prostrate
on stone.

Picture of a Soul

A shirt I was born in.
I wear it. Or it wears me.
White, of course.

A loose fit.
Growing as I grow
but slowly going dull.

It must be washed
once, twice, three times,
then hung to dry.

There, can you see it?
Hanging high
on the hill.

Waving its arms
in the wind. Beckoning.
Sun shining through.

Small Prayer

If my heart were scoured,
    if my soul were remade
into a new and shining garment,
    then would I have to die?

Lord, if perfection is death,
    let me stay here
a little while longer,
    spotted and stained.

House of String

Without hammer or nail,
without planed plank,
I will build a house of string.

One airy room to live in.
String walls, string ceiling
that let the light shine in.

A place to spend the hours
where no clocks ever tick.
Mine alone. Or ours.

O who can understand? O who?
How I have hungered for
the unbuilt, the unimagined.

How a piece of string
trailing me in a long line
wherever I go can be

a sheltering abode, a dwelling
place that is not a place at all.
Come, let us go there now

and sip the tea that is neither
sweet nor bitter, listening
all the while to the crickets

singing. Or not singing.
Safe in its flimsy walls,
we will sleep the sleep

we have always dreamt
of sleeping, rain saturating
our dreams, red leaves

at the door signaling a final fall
where all becomes nothing,
nothing all, where, as soft snow

begins to fall, one of us
will stay and one will go,
walking away from everything

we know, casting a glance
back to a house filling up
with snow, wondering,

O who is the lost one? Who?
The sleeper coldly covered over?
Or the coatless one who leaves

no tracks, who stumbles in the snow?

Snow, the Novel

In the end it was the only story to tell:
snow on the ground and snow silently falling,
the landmarks of a life vanishing, the road
erased, a house half-buried, a watcher watching
from an upper window who knows she cannot
stay and cannot go, she cannot stay or go,
who, as evening falls, withdraws into a dark interior,
feeling her way along the winding corridors
until the deepening snow has overtaken all.

When the last of the last ones go, if I am one
of the last, the last to believe and the last to know,
when Eternity unwrites me, when an unseen hand
lets loose the pen that wrote my story, and directionless,
I step out of the frame into a snowy unfenced field,
my tracks filling up as fast as I can make them,
then will I know the story in its entirety?
Know all that I need to know?
The now that is snow.

Sake

A squat bottle,
two cups, and us
toasting an anniversary
although we know
the wind may blow
away these walls
of paper, wood, and rock;
and if they fall, we'll rise
and quickly improvise
a journey down time's
cold silvery musical stream,
slipping on dripping
stepping-stones, drenched
to the bone until,
shades of our former selves,
we give up the ghost,
our ghastly smiles belying
the cold finality of lying
through centuries side
by side, cheated by time.
What is a marriage?
A promise, a vow never
to forsake the other,
and love a little realm

of light and shadow.
But here, while the sake's
warm. Drink again.
For your sake. Mine.

their light keeps traveling on   it will never darken
forever will it travel   into far reaches   cold corners
farther than light   has ever gone   all the stars that have ever
shone   are shining still   their light doesn't die
no never   the stars assure   in darkness is no peril
like lighthouses   no longer there   stars that went dark
a long time ago   are shining somewhere   their light travels on
something to hold   & keep holding   as we hold on
to ones who have gone on   like lighthouses   no longer there
their light   doesn't die   no never   keeps traveling on
as we stumble   & shine   & remember   looking up

Riddle

You are the bright one,
my dearest possession.
Speechlessly,
you offer up
your pictures:

joy, sorrow, terror, too.
You are both
one and many,
a hoard,
a chest of jewels,

some light-giving,
some taking
the light, until
I lose myself
in darkest night.

O who will perish
first? Me? You?
Though some do,
I pray never
to outlive you.

A Memory of the Future

I will say *tree*, not *pine tree*.
I will say *flower*, not *forsythia*.
I will see *birds*, many *birds*,
flying in four directions.

Then *rock* and *cloud* will be
lost. *Spring* will be lost.
And, most terribly,
your name will be lost.

I will revel in a world
no longer particular.
A world made vague,
as if by fog. But not fog.

Vaguely aware,
I will wander at will.
I will wade deeper
into wide water.

You'll see me, *there*,
out by the horizon,
an old gray thing
who finally knows

gray is the most beautiful color.

My Life

A cracked bowl I hold in my outstretched hands.
A heavy cloak thrown down like a twisted shadow.
A book, its pages full of writing, a few unwritten on.
A book, its pages turning blankly in the wind.
A dream I had once, vanishing as morning comes.
A leaf upturned to the sun.
Rain, rain falling without discrimination.
All this and more so that today I kneel and ask,
Small fish, small silver fish darting in the stream,
   where now are you going?

~~~

Crab

—Again, the dream of prey and predator, I can't remember
when or where, only the pursuit, I am the one pursued,
for minutes, years, until I wake to familiar slanting eaves,
to a ceiling where knotholes look like curious eyes,
and doors hang crooked on their hinges but still are doors.
Once more, by grace or luck, I have escaped capture. I am safe.
Or am I? Now I must navigate the solid world of stairs
steep in their disregard, each thing in this house a *fact* to hold onto.
O yes, to live I must believe in the solidity of this red rocking chair
on a porch in Maine, this cup of coffee steaming in my hand.

                                                            I must believe.

                       ~ ~ ~

The sun is burning off the fog, the islands slowly coming into focus.
A kayak tied to the dock is bobbing gently, a splash of red
in the day's blank canvas. Small boat, I will go out.
I will paddle beyond the seeming solidity of this porch, this house.

                                                               I will go out.

                       ~ ~ ~

Often now I wonder how far can one go, how far?
Horizons exert a pull. Uncountable islands suffer fog's erasures
and then come back. Beneath the water's glossy shifting surface,
traps. Sleek boats in the distance race past unaware,
leaving me bobbing in their wake. The tide takes me out, far out,

the day's debris floating past, a bottle, a buoy,

and one small shipwrecked swimmer expertly skimming

the waves, carried along, or carried away, as I am today.

I scoop it up, small crab, wondering, *Are you alive?*

No. You are dead, dead, dead. You hang, limp and dispirited, in my hand.

A hunger, ravening and unimaginable, has sucked body and soul

out of you through an empty eyehole, leaving your shell intact,

so that you only masquerade as *crab*. O crab, I understand you.

Too often I have done the same.

~ ~ ~

I make you my compatriot for the day. Set you on the bow,

like a figurehead, but facing the wrong way, so that we are eye to eye.

Speak, crab! Be oracle. Interpret the depths of my dream,

the day's dark portents. But you are mute to all entreaty.

You seem to move a claw—*are* you alive?

No, it is only a trick of wind and water. And so I paddle out

to where no cry can be heard from helpless prey or predator.

I cry.

~ ~ ~

The wind is picking up, the sky clouding over into gray.
Waves restless as thoughts that won't stop threaten to swamp me.
I am prey. Return, I must return, or be completely swept away.
Someday I will merge with this landscape supreme in its indifference.

I will be as crab.

~ ~ ~

Leaving this place, another summer gone, I won't
take you with me. I'll leave you facing seaward on the porch railing,
your throne a clamshell, to cast your eye out over islands
leapfrogging to the horizon. I'll say goodbye to a season
quickly disappearing, to a house that only exists in summer, for
summer,
under a spell all winter not to change, to change, to change.
Next summer when I come back, warm flesh and blood
or insubstantial spirit, will you be here to greet me?
Pincer and claw, will you have held on through winter's worst, intact?
O Cyclops, teach me, teach me, teach me, to be dead

and believe in resurrection.

The quotation from Dōgen used by permission of Steven Heine, *Zen Poetry of Dōgen: Verses from the Mountain of Eternal Peace* (Tuttle, 1997).

The answers to the riddles are "ego" and "memory."

"On Riverside Drive": The statue of Shinran Shonin is located at 332 Riverside Drive in Manhattan.

The poem "She Leans" is based on A. Aubrey Bodine's photograph of the same title.

Photo by A. Aubrey Bodine © Jennifer B. Bodine courtesy www.aaubreybodine.com.

Ensō image used by permission of Madison Smartt Bell.

ACKNOWLEDGMENTS

The poems in this book first appeared in the following magazines, online publications, and anthologies:

The American Poetry Review: "Cloud Koan"; "The Sound of the Sea at the Shore"; "My Life"

The Atlantic: "Riddle"; "I"; "A Memory of the Future"; "Small Prayer"; "Small as a Seed"

Ecotone: "Gold Bug"

Five Points: "The Amiable Child"; "On Riverside Drive"; "Enso"

The Hopkins Review: "Snow, the Novel"; "Island Graveyard"

The Hudson Review: "The Streaming"; "Dream Interrupted—"; "Starry Night"

Image: "March: St. John the Divine"

The Iowa Review: "Sake"

Kenyon Review: "Mountains of the Heart"

The New Criterion: "The Shrine"; "Picture of a Soul"

New England Review: "Light Like Water"; "House of String"

Ploughshares: "The Road" (under the title "A Life"); "Constructing a Religion"

Plume: "She Leans"

Poetry: "Pome"

Poetry Daily: "Pome"; "Picture of a Soul"

Transmission (Satellite Press): "Magicicada"

Southwest Review: "Zen Sonnet"

"Riddle" (memory) first appeared in *Alhambra Poetry Calendar 2011* (Alhambra Publishing, Belgium).

"A Memory of the Future" appeared in *Alhambra Poetry Calendar 2013*.

"Constructing a Religion" appeared in the anthology *The Poet's Quest for God* (Eyewear Publishing, London).

I would like to thank Jane Gelfman and Deborah Schneider, friends and agents through many books, and my editor Jill Bialosky for her sustaining belief in these poems. My gratitude also to Phillis Levin for her generous insight and suggestions. And to Madison and Celia who have always been there when I needed their help.

ELIZABETH SPIRES (b. 1952 in Lancaster, Ohio) is the author of six previous collections of poetry: *Globe, Swan's Island, Annonciade, Worldling, Now the Green Blade Rises*, and *The Wave-Maker.*

She has been the recipient of a Whiting Award, a Guggenheim Fellowship, the Amy Lowell Traveling Poetry Scholarship, two fellowships from the National Endowment for the Arts, two Ohioana Book Awards, and the Witter Bynner Prize for Poetry from the American Academy of Arts and Letters. In 2011–12, she was a Cullman Fellow at the New York Public Library. Her poems have appeared in *The Atlantic, The New Yorker, Poetry, American Poetry Review*, and in many other magazines and anthologies, and have been featured on National Public Radio's *The Writer's Almanac.*

She has also written six books for children, including *The Mouse of Amherst, I Am Arachne*, and *I Heard God Talking to Me: William Edmondson and His Stone Carvings.*

She lives in Baltimore and is a professor at Goucher College, where she has taught for many years.